D1127636

Eastern European Poets Series #36

What We Saw from This Mountain: Selected Poems 1976–2014

© Vladimir Aristov, 2017

Introduction, Interview © Julia Trubikhina-Kunina, 2017

Translation © Julia Trubikhina-Kunina, 2017

Eastern European Poets Series #36

Series Editors: Matvei Yankelevich & Rebekah Smith

ISBN 978-1-937027-37-7

First Edition, First Printing, 2017

Ugly Duckling Presse

The Old American Can Factory

232 Third Street #E-303

Brooklyn, NY 11215

www.uglyducklingpresse.org

Distributed in the USA by SPD/Small Press Distribution

Distributed in the UK by Inpress Books

Cover design by Hannah Bardwell

Design and typesetting by Don't Look Now! and Rebekah Smith

The type is Linux Libertine and Gill Sans

Offset printing and binding by McNaughton & Gunn

Covers printed letterpress at Ugly Duckling Presse

Cover paper generously provided by Materials for the Arts

The publisher would like to acknowledge the support of the National
Endowment for the Arts and the New York State Council on the Arts.

ART WORKS. NYSCA

Vladimir Aristov

What We Saw
from This Mountain

Selected Poems 1976–2014

Translated from the Russian by

Julia Trubikhina-Kunina and Betsy Hulick
with contributions from Gerald Janecek,
Rebekah Smith, and Matvei Yankelevich

Edited by Julia Trubikhina-Kunina

Contents

Introduction

What We Saw from This Mountain is the first English-language poetry collection by the contemporary Russian poet, essayist, and prose writer Vladimir Aristov, who lives and works in Moscow, where he was born in 1950. Aristov started writing poetry as a teenager; but, like many of his contemporaries, he was unable to publish before the beginning of Gorbachev's perestroika. His poetry first appeared in 1987 in the well-known literary magazine *Iunost*, along with that of many other poets of his generation whose work became known due to the policies of glasnost: Nina Iskrenko, Evgeny Bunimovich, Ivan Zhdanov, Alexei Parshchikov, Yuriy Arabov, and Sergei Gandlevsky.

Vladimir Aristov's poetry can be situated in a context of late-Soviet unofficial poetry, and is affinitively intertwined with two poets with whom he maintained close friendships for many years: Arkadii Dragomoshchenko (1946–2012), a prolific Leningrad writer and translator, considered the foremost representative of American Language poetry in Russia, and Alexei Parshchikov (1954–2009), a leading figure of the Metarealist poetry movement.

In the early 1980s, Mikhail Epstein and Konstantin Kedrov, among other critics, recognized Parshchikov, Ivan Zhdanov, and Alexander Eremenko as belonging to a movement which they called "Metarealist" or "Meta-metaphorist" (the latter term belonged to Kedrov). These poets were indeed friends and there was a good deal of cross-pollination in their poetry, but they themselves were somewhat skeptical of the terms, pointing to the lack of manifestos and the tendency of critics to create some kind of "Linnaeus' nomenclature" to group writers together. As Epstein noted in his tribute to Parshchikov, "Alyosha's Wittgensteinian family" included and attracted very different poets and artists: Aristov, Dragomoshchenko, Eremenko, Zhdanov, Ilya Kutik, Tatiana Scherbina, the painter Igor Ganikovsky, and others. In

Epstein's words, while Aristov could be seen in some way as overlapping with Dragomoshchenko, Dragomoshchenko with Zhdanov, Zhdanov with Parshchikov, and Parshchikov with Eremenko, Eremenko and Aristov had few similarities. The diverse community was in itself "meta-real"—the relationship was not of group identity but of individual metamorphoses that proceeded in this chain-like manner from one poet to the other. Some poets, such as Dragomoshchenko, dispensed with rhyme altogether, while others, like Parshchikov, worked with conventional Russian verse forms in unconventional ways and with ingenious effectiveness, drawing, for example, on the rhythm and rhymes of syllabic poetry. However, as Eugene Ostashevsky aptly noted when writing about Parshchikov,[1] there were also similarities in the ways these poets dealt with the referentiality of language, in their antimimetic approach to describing reality, and in their affinities with the experiments of American Language poetry, with its emphasis on a multiplicity of voices. Scholars and poets also point out the connection between the baroque aesthetic, and the dynamic complexity, and the mysterious "obscurity" of Metarealist poetry. Mark Lipovetsky, for example, calls the poetry of Zhdanov and Eremenko "neo-baroque."[2] The "baroque" excessiveness of the Metarealist metaphor makes it more than just a poetic trope: the interconnectedness of all things that have no ostensible similarities stretches metaphor to an extreme. Metarealist complexity (syntactical, phonetic, and grammatical) "slows down" reading so as to focus the reader on language itself, making linguistic materiality the primary subject of their poetry.

---

1 Eugene Ostashevsky, "Shkola iazyka, shkola barokko: Alyosha Parshchikov v Kalifornii," *New Literary Observer* 98 (2009): http://magazines.russ.ru/nlo/2009/98/ost32.html.

2 Mark Lipovetsky, "Kontseptualizm i neobarokko," *Ex Libris/NG*, September 9, 2000; N. Leiderman and M. Lipovetsky, *Sovremennaia russkaia literatura* , vol. 3: *V kontse veka (1986-1990)* (Moscow: Academia, 2001), 31–42.

It should also be noted that in the Russian "poetry underground" of the 1970s, the Metarealists diverged from the practices of the Moscow Conceptualist poets, led by Dmitrii Prigov and Lev Rubinstein. While the Conceptualists worked with late Soviet reality and Communist social codes, the Metarealists, each in his own way, worked with multiple realities, their metamorphoses, and a meta-reality of mutual interconnectedness and permeation of both archaic and contemporary cultures. Indeed, after the fall of the Soviet Union, the Conceptualists appeared more rooted in the new, post-communist social environment, while the Metarealists, with their diverse poetics and loose associations based on friendships rather than any articulated ideology, seemed to be more marginalized and dispersed. However, reading the Metarealists' experiments with language and metaphor against the backdrop of today's ever more hybridized and globalized world makes one consider with new appreciation what Ernest Fenolossa wrote a century ago in "The Chinese Written Character as a Medium for Poetry": "The whole delicate substance of speech is built upon substrata of metaphor."[3]

While Parshchikov and Dragomoshchenko are better known in the US, Aristov is of particular interest, as he exemplifies important trends of contemporary Russian poetry—metaphor-centered narrativity, the turn to Language poetry, and the embrace of postmodern theory. Aristov's unmistakable personal style is characterized by both the philosophical thoughtfulness of a lifelong scientist (he has a Ph.D. in Physics and Mathematics and is the author of three books and more than 150 scientific publications) and striking metaphors that evoke the poetry of Osip Mandelstam. Aristov's is sophisticated, intelligent poetry, whose references reach far back, weaving an entire "web" that Russian culture happily—or unhappily—inhabits. Thus "Music," the poem that opens the present collection, by way of a transparent reference to

3 Ernst Fenolossa and Ezra Pound, *The Chinese Written Character as a Medium for Poetry: A Critical Edition*, ed. Haun Saussy, Jonathan Stalling, and Lucas Klein (New York: Fordham University Press, 2008), 54.

Mandelstam's "Silentium," casts further back, to the 1830s, to Tiutchev's "Silentium!"—the infinite recurrence of silence in the already "speechless" world:

> Do not carry away our sound into music,
> For already the sea is so speechless before us,
> Without sound would it grow even more empty?

This tide of repetition in Aristov's poetry—a Nietzschean "eternal return" of sorts, linguistically underscored by his frequent use of "once again," "again," "sometimes,"—is perhaps one of its most significant philosophical features. Canto three of the long narrative poem "Quotidian Immortality" describes a state that is simultaneously "now" and "always":

> I hear your voices beneath the dome of the sea,
> Things among things
> And all my friends...
>
> Like an echo among burning cliffs
> You... and you... and you
>
> [...]
>
> Hasn't the world already known
> Your crystalline eyeglasses
> With their fiery panorama,
> And are they not older than the jellyfish
> Conjured from parachute silk?

In many of Aristov's poems, the sea is the image that harbors both the repetitive tide of coming and going and the namelessness, the pre-sound timelessness, of being. The philosophical embodiment of this simultaneous existence of every thing in its eternal recurrence has been developed and described by Aristov in many essays as *idem-forma*, a concept the definition of which is itself an ongoing process of formulation and re-formulation. *Idem-forma* departs from the idea of the fragmented postmodern world to embrace a unity in which disparate works of art can coexist in a timeless confluence, or mutual integration and penetration, and where the "I," without losing self, can meet and identify with "the Other." And so in the poem, "A Play," a theater director instructs his actors how to perform a legendary meeting between Marina Tsvetaeva and Anna Akhmatova:

> "Impersonating the other
> you hold up your name
> before you as a mask
> but it is the name of another."
> And he gave them sheets of paper
> fastened to long slats
> resembling white fans
> on one he had written
> "Akhmatova" and on the other, "Tsvetaeva"
> "This will make you anonymous doubles"

Ultimately, it seems, Vladimir Aristov's *idem-forma*, as well as the silence that generates all sound and the formlessness that generates all form, also harks back to the romantic and neo-romantic "ineffable." As the nineteenth-century Russian Romantic poet Vasily Zhukovsky says in in his poem "Ineffable," "only silence speaks with clarity." A French contemporary of Zhukovsky, Alphonse de Lamartine, in his poem "Dieu," similarly juxtaposes the language of "*sons articulés*" (articulated sounds) with the other language: "*l'autre, éternel, sublime, universel, immense / Est le langage inné de toute intelligence*" ("the other, eternal, sublime, universal, immense / Is the innate language of all intelligence"). This is a language of primordial universal unity. Being acutely attuned to the post-structuralist fragmentation of the world does not diminish for Aristov the urgency of finding modes of expression for the unity of distant things, of self and other. And this, ultimately, is Vladimir Aristov's poetic quest. To quote further from "A Play":

> ...and whoever made statements
> was actually asking questions
> and was looking at himself
> through the priceless eyes of another...

Julia Trubikhina-Kunina
New York, August 2016

What We Saw
from This Mountain

Музыка

Как выбрал ты священные листки,
Обернутые в нотные прожилки?
Есть правильные звуки в мире сем,
Ты вынул их из мира,
И место поросло, как не бывало

Остались пустыри и бред каменоломен,
Небесных пуговиц сухая синева
На ватниках в кирпичных терриконах,
Лишь дратва уст, кустов, пересечений
Далеких еле всхолмленных небес,
Все заросло, все заросло до слез.

Как отгрузить нам хладобойный век,
С горы спускаясь в ледяном вагоне,
С откоса заблудившейся травы
Во мрак земли и тишину объятий.

О позабытом плещет тишина,
Не уходи, эпоха неолита,
С ружьем, направленным в простор реки,
С исчезновеньем поворота жизни
За блещущим колесиком воды,
Где вспухшее крыло стеклянной птицы
Подъято вверх циничной силой мысли.

Метеоритов век не наступил,
Еще подобные деревьям или людям
От сладостной земли не устремились камни,
Еще равнины нам принадлежат,
И волчий след наполнен талым слепком.

Music

How did you choose the sacred scores
Wrapped in sinuous notes?
There are true sounds in this world,
You took them from the world,
And the place grew over, as if it had never been.

All that remain are wastelands and ravings of quarries,
The desiccated blue of heaven's buttons
On quilted jackets in heaps of broken brick,
Only a waxen thread of lips and shrubs, and crossings
Of distant, barely hummocked skies,
Everything overgrown, all overgrown to tears.

How can we unload the dead cold era,
Descending a mountain on an icy train,
Along slopes of errant grass,
Into the darkness of earth and the silence of embraces.

The silence splashes about all that's forgotten
Don't leave us, Neolithic era
With a rifle aimed at the vastness of the river,
With life's turning point vanishing
Behind a shining wheel of water,
Where the swollen wing of a glass bird
Is lifted up by thought's cynical power.

It is not yet the age of the meteorites,
Still rocks, like trees or people,
Have not yet lifted away from blissful earth,
The plains are still ours,
And wolf tracks are cast in melting snow.

В открытое окно пустынный двор земли
Доносит голоса под полнолуньем,
Но этот мерный хаос впрячь не удалось
Ни в звездные цирюльные пустоты,
Ни в города глубокого гранита.

Не уноси же в музыку наш звук,
И так безмолвно море перед нами,
Без звука разве больше опустеет?
Не надо музыки, не надо звезд
Пред нашим древним морем без названий.

1977

Beneath a full moon voices carry
Through the open window from Earth's empty courtyard,
But we cannot harness this measured chaos
Neither to the voids of stars and shaving foam,
Nor to the cities of deep granite.

Do not carry away our sound into music,
For already the sea is speechless before us.
Without sound would it grow even more empty?
There is no need for music, no need for stars
In front of our ancient, nameless sea.

JT / BH / MY

5

Треугольный пакет молока.
Если угол обрежешь,
То белая хлынет тоска.
Как письмо непрочитанное
Пропадает в ночи.
Тихо. Молчи.

На росе разведенный,
Рассвет, помутившись, растет
За углом, где работа постылая ждет.
Я его позабыла,
Значит в памяти он никогда не умрет.

На окне на ночном цветных пирамид молока
Громоздятся мучные бока.
Молока струйку зыбкую чувствуя нить –
Эту память уже не прервать, не продлить.

1979

from the cycle "From Someone Else's Life"

Triangular packet of milk.
If you cut off the corner,
White melancholy will pour out.
Like a letter unread
That disappears in the night.
Hush. Be quiet.

Diluted with dew,
The sunrise clouds over, expanding
Around the corner, where the job you loathe is waiting.
I've forgotten him, she says,
Which means in memory he'll never die.

The colored pyramids of chalky milk
Pile up on the window at night.
Feeling the trickling flow of milk, this thread,
This memory can neither be cut off, nor drawn out.

JT / BH

Занятия археологией

Откуда знаю я, что живы мы?
Как отличить мне месиво живое
От Геркуланума пустот?

И я ходил по берегам реки,
Вступал в людские разговоры
И любовался первозданной формой,
Готовой стать иль домом иль дворцом

Под трактором холодные бо́розды
На грязи свежей раннего литья
Запечатлеть, выпарывая ветошь
Из темной телогрейки под кустом

Едва сдувать оранжевую пыль с ресниц,
Окрашенных египетскою охрой,
И цвета синего дворового заката
Ткань рубчатую собрать со всех.

Не сверху у ворот в Микенах
Заглядывать сквозь толщу ила,
Но снизу сквозь решетку тротуара
Сухого пресного под львиными вратами
Решеток бывших английского клуба
Читать о распорядке ночи: да, закрыто по субботам.

Писать об этом можно без конца:
Ведь свиток я пишу и сам читаю:
Как в подворотнях довоенный шепот
И хвойный трубный голос роз военных
И сон послевоенных мавзолеев,
Когда чтобы через болото перебраться,
На ичиги прикручивают генеральские погоны.
Не торопиться в описи вещей,

Exercises in Archaeology

How do I know we are living?
How to distinguish the living mess of flesh
From the empty spaces left in Herculaneum?

And I walked along the riverbanks
Made small talk with the people
And admired the original form
That either house or palace would become.

To press cold furrows in the fresh
Morning mud left by a tractor's
Passage, tearing the batting from
A quilted jacket under a shrub.

To barely blow orange dust from lashes
Rimmed with Egyptian ochre,
To gather from each waled fabric
The blue of courtyard sunsets.

To gaze through the thickness of silt,
Not from above by the gate in Mycenae,
But from below through the grate in the dry,
Insipid sidewalk, under the lion's gate,
The former grate of the English Club
To read the night's schedule: yes, closed Saturdays.

One could write about this endlessly:
I write on a scroll that I alone read:
Like a prewar whisper in back alleys,
The coniferous, trumpeting voice of wartime roses
And the dream of postwar mausoleums,
When generals' epaulets are fastened
Onto Tatar boots in order to cross the swamp.
Not to rush the inventory of things,

(Себя не позабыть среди других...)
Рукопожатий крепких, как цемент,
И поцелуев — пятен на граните,
Сверканий тех огней иллюминальных
И ненависти безымянных дней.

Всем зорким старческим дыханием дышать,
Чтобы не пыль,— пыльца золотозмейки
По правую бы руку отходила
И становилась тяжестью земной.

1977

(Not to forget oneself among others...)
Strong handshakes like cement,
And kisses like flecks on granite,
The sparkle of those celebratory lights,
And the hatred of nameless days.

To breathe with the farsighted breath of the old
So that it's not mere dust, but golden serpent's dust
That would fly off to the right
To become the weight of the earth.

JT / BH

Изыскатели
(30-е годы)

Перед нами земля открывалась,
Где живое еще не враждебно живому.

Темным утром открылась Сибирь,
Ржа́вень светлая лиственниц
В долину парящую шла.
И с обрыва гранитной горы
Нам нельзя было сдвинуть незнакомое тело
В огромную чуждую жизнь.

Что мы видели с этой горы
Под небом, полным замерзшего жара,
Забывая материю предвоенную нашей одежды.
Как мы счастливы были в земле этой.
И нет нам прощенья.

Почему же глаза закрыв,
Мы не видим, как тени земные сошлись
В разделенных равнинах.
Ждет возлюбленную немецкий офицер
У Бранденбургских ворот,
Погрузив лицо свое мертвое в берлинские розы.

Почему же так страшно сердцу здесь,
Ведь оно не в перекрестках дорог
Предвоенной Европы,
Где загнанные в холодной росе
Молоком поят локомобили.

В лихорадочном блеске ногтей
Снимаются копии полей ночных,

The Prospectors
(1930s)

Ahead of us a land unfurled to be discovered,
Where the living was not yet enemy to the living.

One dark morning, Siberia was opened up,
The bright rust of larches
Moved into the soaring valley.
And from the cliff of a granite mountain
We could not budge the unknown body
Into a vast and alien life.

What we saw from this mountain
Under a sky full of frozen heat,
Forgetting the prewar fabric of our clothing.
How happy we were in this land.
And there is no forgiveness for us.

Why then, with eyes closed,
Can't we see that earthly shadows have converged
In the divided lowlands?
A German officer waits for his beloved
At the Brandenburg Gate,
Plunging his dead face into Berlin roses.

Why then is the heart so frightened here,
If, after all, it's not at the crossroads
Of prewar Europe,
Where, driven to exhaustion in the cold dew,
Locomobiles are given milk to drink.

In the feverish brilliance of fingernails
Copies are made of fields at night,

Аэродромы спящих стрекоз
И стоянки цветов полевых.

Смутным запахом мокнет табачным
И знакомую пыль предзакатно кружѝт
За фабричной стеною «Дуката»,
Кожаный воздух сминая смолистый
С курткой у кирпичной и черной стены.
Открывается дверь, и за вышедшим человеком
Он уходит туда, поближе к закату,
Тот оглянется и повернется опять:
Перелески зеленые солнц
И пожарные лестницы неба
Проходят в последний путь над головой,
Под небом далеким скрываясь.

Кто же нам скажет, какою платить нам ценой,
Ведь мы отыскали долину,
Что идет к океану в бесконечной своей прямизне.

Но пробившись через гранит,
Мы и здесь человека открыли —
Человека наших годов.
Мы стояли пред завещанным тайным стеклом,
Апельсиновым деревом там стекал человек,
Закрывал от света глаза
И у камня просил он прощенья.

Завиднелось далекое царство без сна,
В халцедоновых светлых долинах
Стояла ночная вода.
Открывались дремучие ставни осеннего камня,
И танталовой грудью пространства
Звенела рабочая мгла.

Airfields of sleeping dragonflies
And encampments of wildflowers.

A vague smell of tobacco wets the leathery air
That whirls familiar pre-sunset dust
Behind the Ducat cigarette factory,
Tar-like, and creasing a jacket
By the black and brick wall.
A door opens and it follows the emerging man
Moving in the same direction, closer to the sunset;
He'll look around and turn again:
Green coppices of suns
And fire escapes of sky
Pass by on their final journey overhead,
Hiding behind distant heavens.

Who will then tell us what price to pay,
For we've searched out the valley
That leads to the ocean, in its infinite straightness,

But after breaking through the granite,
We've discovered humankind here as well—
A man of our age.
We stood before the secret glass we inherited;
There, like an orange tree, a man sliding down,
Shielding his eyes from the light
And asking forgiveness of the stone.

A sleepless kingdom glimmered in the distance,
And the nighttime water stood still
In the bright Chalcedonian valleys.
The drowsy shutters of autumn stone opened slowly
And the dark throng of workers breathed
With the Tantalus-lungs of space.

Опустись на колени в кремнистом ручье.
Пресной ряби пустырь
И вересковый ветр понаслышке.
Все гудит молотков полевой перезвон.

Только гром мы услышим
Уходящих во глубь поездов,
Но и только... и хрипы ночной пересмены.
Не разбудят во тьме голоса.
Только рокот и шепот и смерть
И гром пробуждающих поездов.

1976–1977

Get down on your knees in the flintstone creek.
A desert of freshwater ripples
And heather wind by hearsay.
Field-chimes of hammers drone on.

We'll hear only the thunder
Of trains leaving for the depths,
But only that... and the wheezing of the night shift.
Voices will not wake us in the dark.
Only the rattle and whisper and death
And thunder of awakening trains.

JT / BH / MY

17

О дай мне жалости к дракону,
Пока он спит,
И диктор шепчет равнодушным словом
Его дневную речь.
Покуда он не пробудился,
В глазах кровавые глубины не открылись.
Пока Георгий не пришел,
Свое копье не погрузил
В бессильный глаз.
Пока от боли дракон не стал столь человечным.
Дай мне успеть, покуда жив Георгий.
И диктор не способен в страхе
Летучей мыши сквозь себя полет сдержать
И в воздух словом отпускает.

1980

from the cycle "Historical Commentaries"

O grant me pity for the dragon
While he sleeps
And the radio announcer's voice whispers indifferently
His daytime speech.
Before the dragon wakes
Before the bloody depths have opened in his eyes
Before St. George appears
To plunge his spear
Into that defenseless eye.
Before the dragon has become so human in his pain.
O grant me time enough while St. George lives.
And the announcer is unable in his fright
To forestall the flight of the bat piercing him
And lets it go into the air as a word.

JT / BH

К посещению Бахом столицы Пруссии
Берлина в 1747 году

Неотделимо тело от парика,
Неотличима зеркальная гладь реки
От завитков зеленоватых трав.

На что мне добротный костюм,
Он и так запыленный лежит,
Словно старый конверт на дне светлой реки
В одна тысяча девятьсот сорок седьмом году.

Не надо и створкой зеркальной кареты
Лучик чужой ловить,
Чтобы светить в себя,
Ведь в камере-обскуре забытой
Все свалены в смехотворных позах,
И кровь девятнадцатого столетья
Похожа ныне на желе для бритья.

Кто подскажет мне как мне быть,
Если тело всего лишь храм,
Кто нашепчет мне в уши
Улицей зеленоватой
Королевскую тему и шестиголосный канон.

Как белесая медь вокруг разлита...
И в березах бирюзовая сыпь на запястьях.
Ты ли думаешь, что возьмешь меня
Гулом чугунным, идущим из ноздрей коня?
Как посылку для века небудущего схороня
И химической надписью
Поджигая в воздухе, отошлешь поклон.

Немота стены из зеркальных линз реки бирюзовой.

1983

On the Occasion of Bach's Visit to Berlin, Capital of Prussia, in 1747

Inseparable, the body from the wig,
Indiscernible, the smooth reflection of the river
From the greenish curls of grass.

Why do I need a well-made suit,
Which anyway lies dusty
Like an envelope at the bottom of a clear river
In the year one thousand nineteen hundred and forty-seven?

No need to catch a stranger's sunbeam
In the window of a prismatic carriage
To shine into yourself
For in the forgotten camera obscura
Everyone heaped in ridiculous poses,
And the blood of the nineteenth century
Nowadays resembles shaving gel.

Who can advise me of what to do
If the body is only a temple,
Who will whisper in my ears
By way of a greenish street
The royal theme and six-voiced canon?

As if pale copper were spilled all over...
A turquoise rash on the wrists of birches,
Do you really think you could get me
With the cast-iron din from the horse's nostril?
As if storing a parcel for a century never to be
Emblazoning the air with a chemical signature,
You send off your greetings.

In the mirroring lens of a turquoise river, the muteness of a wall.

JT / BH / RS / MY

21

из поэмы «Бессмертие повседневное» (Часть 3)

Голоса мне слышны ваши из-под купола моря,
Вещи вещей
И друзья мои все…

Будто эхо меж скал раскаленных:
Ты… и ты… и ты
Голоса, замершие в августовской тишине,
Словно дымный медузы листик вянущий

Как же назвать мне вас,
Чтобы вы погрузились во врéмя,
Чтобы ты не ушла из него однажды
                с гремящею галькой подножья?

Разве очки твои хрусталевидные
С огненной панорамой
Не были раньше в мире
И не старше медуз,
Созданных из парашютного шелка?

Разве не дети твоих волос золотистых
Деревья остроконечные эти?
И генуэзской крепости холм над летним плечом твоим

Слово молчит,
И время между иллюминаторов спит.
Серою цифровою медузой
Безвидный корабль слепит свой защитный торс.

Влагой иной и пыльцою пронизаны
                бабочки крылья фанерного
                у выхода сада морского…

from "Quotidian Immortality" (Canto 3)

I hear your voices from beneath the dome of the sea,
Things among things
And all my friends...

Like an echo among burning cliffs:
You... and you... and you
Voices silenced in August quiet
The wilting leaf of a jellyfish, the color of smoke

How am I to give you a name
So that you sink deep into time
So that you do not one day escape it
                    gravel rumbling under your feet?

Hasn't the world already known
Your crystalline eyeglasses
With their fiery panorama,
And are they not older than the jellyfish
Conjured from parachute silk?

Are not these trees with their sharp endpoints
The children of your golden hair?
The rise of Genoa's fortress above your summer shoulder

The word is speechless
And time sleeps between portholes.
Like a gray, digital jellyfish
The sightless ship blinds its armored torso.

Otherworldly moisture and dust saturate
          a butterfly's wings at the exit
          of the plywood marine garden...

И никуда не отписаться
От воды с прозрачной щекой
Под плоскою мискою денег...

И чебреца расписка в безвременьи слова.

1981—1984

And there is no getting away
With your transparent cheek
Touching the water under a beggar's bowl...

And in the timelessness of the word, a receipt of wild thyme.

JT / BH

25

Дельфинарий

(Стихотворение в четырнадцати высказываниях)

Посвящается Оружейным баням

*Дельфин — морское млекопитающее
из подотряда зубатых китов,
служит предметом промысла,
его сало идет на выработку жиров,
шкура дает прочную кожу,
плавники и хвост — клей.*

Словарь иностранных слов, 1954 г.

Let us go then, you and I...

— T.S. Eliot,
«The Love Song of J. Alfred Prufrock»

I

Ну что ж, пойдем,
Ты и я...

И в переулке
За водной гладью воздуха
Расстанемся
Здесь по сторонам решетки,
Где кладбище осенних самолетов —
Обезображенной случайно кленовой жести.

Ты скрылся в последнюю арку,
И я губы обвел изнутри языком,
И язык мой недвижно лег,
К зубам припав головою.

Ты мелькнул, как дельфин со свирепым лицом,
С огоньком сигареты

The Dolphinarium
(A Poem in Fourteen Statements)

Dedicated to the Armory Baths

Dolphin—a sea mammal from the
Subclass of toothed whales,
Serves as an object of trade;
Its fat is used to produce lard,
Its skin provides durable leather,
Its fins and tail provide glue.

Dictionary of Foreign Words, 1954

Let us go then, you and I...

— T.S. Eliot,
"The Love Song of J. Alfred Prufrock"

I

Well then, let's go,
You and I...

And in the sidestreet
Beyond the smooth water of the air
We'll part
Here, on either side of this fence
Of accidentally disfigured maple tinplate,
Where there's a cemetery for airplanes of autumn.

You concealed yourself in the last archway,
And I circled the inside of my lips with my tongue,
And my tongue lay motionless,
Resting its head on my teeth.

You appeared for a flash like a dolphin with a ferocious face,
With a cigarette flame

Уходя ночною Москвою.
И язык мой, блеснув,
Ушел вглубь меня,
Пробираясь по крови
С фонариком речи.

Выходи на поверхность, дельфин,
Это тело твое проступило во тьме
Еще ранних сырых переулков,
И из влажной глуби
Твоей и моей
Шел голос морской.

Стрекотал в фонтане дельфин
С медным плещущим мундштуком во рту,
Застыв перед входом
У зашторенных иллюминаторов глаз.

II

Кто слышал крик дельфина?

Я не слышал...

Кто дешифровывал в ночи их голоса
Из влажной донаучной тьмы
Родного переулка,
Кто с ними говорил на эсперанто междометий?

И погружаясь с головою
В поддельные осциллограммы
Их голос на руках вздымал?
Но разве мы там его ищем?

Плещется в нас ночной дельфинарий,
Не усидеть у окошек его.

Receding in the Moscow night.
And my tongue flashed
Then sank into my depths,
Cutting a path through my blood
With the flashlight of speech.

Come to the surface, dolphin;
This body of yours has emerged from the dark
Of damp still early sidestreets,
And from the humid deep
Of you and of me
Rose the voice of the sea.

A dolphin chattered in the fountain
A splashing brass mouthpiece in its beak,
Stood still before the entrance
Near the shuttered portholes of eyes.

II

Who heard the cry of the dolphin?

Not I...

Who spent nights deciphering their voices
From the moist pre-scientific dark
Of a sidestreet back home,
Who spoke to them in the Esperanto of interjections?

And who drowned themselves completely
In counterfeit oscillograms,
Raising armfuls of their voice?
But is that where we'll find it?

A nighttime dolphinarium plashes inside us:
You can't stay by its windows for long.

Выйдем к внешнему морю,
Где мы плыли без глаз.
Где оголенные спали
У раскаленных вод
И нараспев считали
Длинный перечень лет.

Ах эти бани —
Вот наш забытый сад морской...
Как описать их?

В предбанной ночи сохнут полотенца,
Их махровые пальцы залетают в мир,
И мыло прижав к самой груди,
По переулкам шли мы, как в мастерские.

Мастеровые или лингвисты
С языками, спрессованными из бронзовых
                          мелких опилок,
Все мы стеклись во тьме в Оружейные бани.

III

Застенчивая прелесть Оружейного
Я твои стены, видно, больше не увижу —
Строительная пыль развеяна
Над пыльным зеркалом, живущим в каждой луже.

Дельфины жили в Оружейной бане,
Но краны им, наверно, перекрыли,
Напрасно собирались на собранье,
Его, как видно, так и не открыли.

Осталась деревянная решетка
Того торжественного трапа,

Let's go out to the external sea
Where we swam without eyes.
Where naked we slept
By the burning waters.
We counted in song
The inventory of years.

Ah, these baths—
Here's our forgotten marine garden...
How to describe them?

In the dressing room of night the towels are drying.
Their terrycloth fingers fly into the world,
And holding the soap to our chests
Down sidestreets we walked, as if to the workshop.

Artisans or linguists
With tongues compressed of fine
                    brass filings,
In the dark we flowed together to the Armory Baths.

III

O bashful charms of Armory Alley,
Your walls, it seems, I'll see no more:
Above the dusty mirror that lives in every puddle
The construction dust has been scattered to the winds.

Dolphins lived in the Armory Bath
But their water, no doubt, has been shut off.
In vain they gathered for the meeting,
For clearly, it would never commence.

Only the wooden grating remains
Of that splendid staircase

Куда в священный пар звала побудка
От переулочного храпа.

Я с вами пиво пил, хоть времени в обрез,
Я прошептал сквозь пену общежитья,
Что мы окружены водой и кровью,
Но по кафельным плитам вода уже не бежит,
И сух дельфинарий.

IV

Лает в наушниках море
Над паутиной волны,
Кто там хрипит или молит...

Что там, детский призыв
Или родительский голос...
Кто же тебя заставит
Перевести их лениво
В доли речи ничьей
И музыкой проложить:

«Сынок, космическая глина,
На ощупь мы тебя лепили
Под тенью быстрого дельфина,
Над темью дна
И под качнувшейся лазурью
В безбрежность отпускали сына.»

Или:

«Словно пух, мы бросали тебя под солнце,
Где томимая светом вода,
Не затем, чтоб торпедой свинцовой
Уходил ты громить города.

Toward which a reveille summoned
The snoring sidestreet into the sacred steam.

I drank beer with you, though time was short,
And I whispered through the communal foam
That we are surrounded by water and blood,
But water no longer runs down the tiled steps,
And the dolphinarium is dry.

IV

The sea barks in my earphones
Over the spiderweb of a wave,
Who wheezes there or pleads...

What is it, a child calling out
Or a parent's voice...
Who will force you
To translate them lazily
Into sections of no one's speech
And cut a path with music:

"My son, cosmic clay,
We molded you by touch alone
Beneath the shadow of a speeding dolphin,
Above the darkness of the sea floor
Beneath the shaken azure
Releasing you, our son, into the boundless."

Or:

"Like feathery down, we tossed you into the sun,
Where the water is wearied by light,
But not so you would go forth
As a leaden torpedo to sack cities.

И вот стоишь ты и не знаешь,
Где утопить свою главу...
Здесь, где отхлынули улицы
На перекрестке сухом.

Замер ты,
Заглядевшись на площадь,
Где гений твой на пьедестале
Повернулся вослед уходящему солнцу,
Опершись на каменную гитару...»

Теперь я и сам увидал его.
Но все разошлись в парикмахерские —
Растворились в пульверизаторах пыли ночной,
А ты дельфин один на пилке зубов играешь
У входа в разбитые бани.

V

Кто обезвоженным ртом мычал
С подводным тремоло созвучий,
Кто с бубенцом транзистора
Похмельною мотая головою,
Брел на водопой —
Тот поймет тебя.

Тебя молодой дельфин,
Заблудившегося в переулках,
Я увидел – ты подслушивал тайно себя
Через провод, идущий к ушам,
Куда поджелудочный магнитофон напевал
Сквозь стальные кассеты свои.

Это он твой гитарный кумир
Шептался с тобой у самой воды,

And now you stand and do not know
Where to drown your head...
Here, where the streets have ebbed
At a dry crossroads.

You stood still,
Staring off at the open square,
Where your genius on a pedestal,
Leaning against a stone guitar,
Turned to follow the waning sun..."

Now I too have seen him.
But everyone has gone off to their barbershops,
Has dissolved in the pulverizers of night's dust,
And you, lone dolphin, play on a tooth saw
At the entrance to the ruined baths.

V

He whose dried-out mouth bellowed
In an underwater tremolo of consonances,
Who, head lolling, hungover,
With the jingle of a transistor radio
Staggered to the watering hole—
He will understand you.

I saw you, young dolphin
Lost in the side streets,
Secretly eavesdropping on yourself
With a wire winding its way to your ears,
Into which the tape recorder, subgastric, sang
With its steel cassettes.

It was he, your guitar idol,
Who whispered with you at the very water's edge,

Вызывая тебя из моря.
Ведь когда-то и он
Гитарный атлет
В беспорядочной мира пальбе
Все ясней проступал изваяньем из вод
И отбросив прозрачные створы,
Замер над миром.

Там в воде отражаясь,
Перемигивались городские огни,
И красные глазки дельфинов
Скрывались в морское метро.

Но в мерцающих искрах одежды сухой
Из расколотой бани ни звука,
И сух ваш летний ночной дельфинарий,
И пуст ваш ночной дельфинарий.

VI

Кто ты вставший и певший,
Чтоб нас судить?

Если ты гитарный бог
В безводную ночь
С ними заговоришь просто на их родном языке...

Но они при виде тебя
Закрывают уши,
Так что камфора капельками выступает.

И ты застывший ничего им не сможешь сказать
На языке океанских наречий,
Ты, снявший маску бога морского,
Ведь сух дельфинарий.

Summoning you from the sea.
For at one time he, too,
A guitar athlete
In the disorderly worldwide barrage,
Ever more clearly emerging as a sculpture in water,
Threw open the transparent casements,
Stood still over the world.

There, reflected in the water,
The city lights flickered to each other
And little red dolphin eyes
Disappeared into the subway of the sea.

Not a sound in the shimmering sparks
Of dry clothing from the gutted bathhouse.
Dry is your summer night dolphinarium,
Empty your night dolphinarium.

VI

Who are you who stood up and sang
That you should judge us?

If you, guitar god,
In the waterless night
Were simply to chat with them in their native tongue...

But at the sight of you
They shut their ears
So that camphor comes out in droplets.

And you, standing still, can say nothing to them
In the language of ocean dialects,
You, who took off your sea god's mask.
For dry is the dolphinarium.

VII

Повернись же к себе
И в себя вглядись...
Кто ты там за очами своими сухими?

Вспомни, к городу ты подъезжал,
Что вечерний темнел на горе,
И, признайся, сильнее руками ты сжал
Поручень бархатный в коридоре вагона.

Там на холме ты стоял
В рост неземной,
Достойный, ты думал, для человека.

И как будто друзья твои разом заговорили
                в поезда броневом стекле,
И радостью светились медальные блики их лиц,
И резные листья заката
Облепили твое лицо.

Так тебя воздвигали...

И когда закатное солнце втянуло, казалось,
                всю кровь с плеч твоих,
Ты увидел,
Что лишь между статуй своих ты стоял.

Так тебя добивали
Верноподданные твои.

Дайте крови моей, ты шептал,
Дайте крови!

И рассыпал лишь горсть чешуи,
Прикоснувшись к своей улыбке.

VII

So, turn to yourself
And look within...
Who are you in there behind your dry eyes?

Remember, you were approaching the city,
That evening city growing dark on the mountain,
And, admit it, you tightened your grip
On the velvet handrail in the train car corridor.

There on the hill you stood tall
Of unearthly height,
Worthy, you thought, of a person.

It's as though your friends all at once started talking
                in the bulletproof window of the train,
And the medallion glints of their faces shone with joy,
And the carved leaves of the sunset
Plastered your face.

Thus they exalted you in bronze...

And when the setting sun, it seemed, had sucked all the
                blood from your shoulders,
You saw
That you were standing only among your own statues.

Thus were you done in
By your faithful followers.

Bring me my blood, you whispered,
Bring me blood!

And you merely scattered a handful of scales
Once you had touched your own smile.

Но далекие башни больших городов
О забытой ночи напоминали,
Где над рекой
Любимая твоя прошла.

VIII

Она тогда тебя искала,
Поверь мне...

Прошла она под арками ночными,
Где ветер, словно легкая косынка
    притягивал к себе ее земное платье.

И замерла под тенью серой мо́ста,
Переступив на лестнице гранитной,
Чтоб вытряхнуть из туфли летнюю былинку.

И видела за темною рекою
На гребнях крыш туманных часовых
С осыпавшейся тяжкою пыльцою
От каменных венков колосовых.

Над набережной ты покачнулась
И поплыла над окнами у замершей воды
И над всеми лицами в сиреневой пыльце.

Но лишь одного тебя она искала,—
Ты спал здесь между статуй
С румянцем мрачным на лице.

Ты рубиконы рук переходила
По стынущим часам с запястий,
Ты промежутки лиц переплывала.

But the distant towers of big cities
Recalled the forgotten night,
Where above the river
Your beloved passed by.

VIII

She was searching for you then,
Believe me...

She passed beneath the nighttime archways
Where the light kerchief of the wind
        drew to itself her earthly dress.

Stepping over a granite stair,
She stopped in the gray shadow of the bridge
To shake from her shoe a blade of summer grass.

And on the crests of fog-shrouded roofs
Beyond the dark river, she saw sentries;
Their stone garlands of wheat
Shed heavy pollen.

Above the embankment she swooned for a moment
And swam above the windows near the stilled water
And over all the faces in the lilac pollen.

But she was looking for you alone—
You were sleeping here among the statues
With a gloomy flush on your cheek.

She crossed Rubicons of arms
Along bestilled wristwatches,
She swam the gaps between their faces.

И над сияньем умершим остановилась,
Застыв на облаке
Над образом лица.

А ты не видел ее, а ты покинул ее...
Ни дельфины и ни тритоны
Не трубили в пустую ночь.

Ты увидел, как за шахматной далью паркета
Между карликовых нежных лимонных деревьев
Ты ушел, поклонившись,
Шагом шахматного коня.

Оглянувшись, ты вынул ключ из груди.

IX

Впрочем, зачем тосковать...
Остановись,
Еще шаг...

Можно теперь прикурить.

С оголенным лицом
Пред ощерившимися дискозубами
Что кричать, что петь?

Это ты еще с высоты пьедестала
Стоял и завистливым оком
Взирал на людей и дельфинов.

И вы готовились слушать,
Уже не терзаясь предсмертно
Ночным расставаньем с водой.

And above the dying glow she stopped,
Stood still on a cloud
Above the image of a face.

But you did not see her, and you abandoned her...
Neither dolphins nor tritons
Trumpeted into the empty night.

You saw that, beyond the chessboard distance of the parquet
Amidst the tender dwarf lemon trees,
You had bowed and walked away
In a knight's move.

Glancing around, you took the key from inside your breast.

IX

On the other hand, why be sad...
Stop,
One more step...

Now you can get a light and smoke.

What can you shout, what can you sing
With a naked face
Before bared disk-teeth?

That was you still at the height of a pedestal
You stood with envious eye,
Gazed at people and dolphins.

And you were preparing to listen,
No longer tormenting yourselves before the death
Of night's separation from water.

Расселись дельфины по голым трибунам,
Говоря на языке зажигалок
И трением кожи о кожу.

X

Зачем голодные смеющиеся рты
Рассеялись по всей долине,
Расселись по водам и весям,
Вы перевесясь, никните на проводах,
Дельфины,
Зачем вы слушаете меня?

Скажите!
Ну!
Прошу вас!

Но вы припали в страхе к телу друга
И слушаете, слушаете, слушаете:
Как за грудной решеткой бьется сердце.

Но почему не слышите, о чем пою я вам?

XI

Все мы станем сиамскими братьями,—
Вены скрестим друг с другом,—
Чтобы общая кровь в морских виноградниках
Нас обняла леонардовым кругом.

А ты сквозь очки скользнул под воду,
Ты лицо раскрыл и в испуге дельфина
                вокруг ты видишь,

The dolphins sat down on bare bleachers,
Speaking the language of cigarette lighters
And by rubbing skin against skin.

X

Why did hungry, laughing mouths
Scatter themselves over the whole valley,
Sit down over land and water,
Leaning over, you go limp on the wires,
Dolphins,
Why are you listening to me?

Tell me!
Go on!
I ask you!

But, in fear, you pressed yourself to the body of a friend
And you listen, listen, listen:
How the heart beats behind the grille of ribs.

But why don't you hear of what I sing to you?

XI

We will all become Siamese twins—
Cross our veins with each other's—
So that the common blood in the vineyards of the sea
Would enclose us in Leonardo's circle.

Through goggles you slipped beneath the water,
You uncovered your face and in fright you see
                a dolphin around,

Там в другом — иная твоя свобода,
Но ты себя ненавидишь?

Это не ты... это не мы — перемол морзянки,
Хруст во рту от стеклянных знаков.
Но больше нельзя, нельзя, нельзя
Кричать в ночную сушь,
Оступаясь скользя
В свою неизвестную глушь.

XII

Что спеть еще вам напоследок,
Сходя в морскую глушь?
Давя ногой ракушки
Наушников и телефонов?

Но почему, скажи, дельфин,
В наушниках ты вечно,
И я тебя не понимаю?

Что шепчут тебе в стоптанные уши,
Когда лежишь на пыльной мостовой,
Беруши?

Куда идешь ты?
Зачерпывая финики с лотков,
Мелькая черным бантиком хвоста?

Следи, дельфин,
Как чертит море караван судов,
Разыскивая карие провалы
В кофейной жиже мира.

There, in another—your other freedom,
But do you hate yourself?

It's not you... it's not us—the fine grind of Morse code,
The crunch of glass symbols in the mouth,
But you can no longer, no longer, no longer
Shout into the night's dryness,
As you stumble, slipping
Into your unknown depths.

XII

What else shall I sing to you in closing?
Descending into the depths of the sea?
Crushing underfoot the shells
Of earphones and telephones?

But tell me, dolphin, why
Are you always coming in through earphones,
And why don't I understand you?

The earplugs—
What do they whisper in your worn-out ears
When you lie on the dusty pavement?

Where are you going,
Scooping up dates from the fruit stands,
The black bow of your tail flashing?

Observe, dolphin,
How the caravan of ships charts the sea,
Seeking out brown chasms
In the coffee-colored mire of the world.

И кто-то на моторке
Пускается один
С эсхатолотом блуждать над морем.

Ужель ты ждешь,
Когда под вопль аплодисментов
И магния бесшумные круги
Корабль с подводной бульбой вместо носа
Ты за собою повлечешь
В наполненную минами авоську,
Чтобы подняв ее ликуя,
Взлететь уныло над толпой?

Иди, дельфин,
Ни слов, ни букв не ведай,
Плыви в раскатах раковин квартирных.

Пока вода не пришла
Для опустевших душей ночных.

XIII

Если ночью вода войдет,
Опустевшие души прольются горячим дождем.

И вы застывшие по банным полка́м,
По кафельным по́лкам
Понахохлившись, в мыле по бро́ви
Отгребете руками радугу пены
   К ступеням у входа.

Вы скользнете кафельным глянцем
В источимой тоске,
И отпущенный пар сойдет
Над открывшимся чистым морем.

And someone in a motorboat
Sets out alone
With an eschatometer to roam over the sea.

Do you really expect,
To the roar of applause
And the noiseless circles of magnesium flashbulbs,
That you will pull a ship behind you,
With a submerged bulb in place of a prow,
Into a string bag full of mines
And, lifting it up, triumphant,
Fly despondently over the crowd?

Go, dolphin,
Know neither words nor letters,
Swim in the peals of kitchen seashell sinks.

Until the water comes
To fill deserted showers of the night.

XIII

If the water enters in the night,
The deserted showers will spill out boiling rain.

And, motionless on bathhouse benches,
Hunched on tiled ledges,
Soaped up to the eyebrows,
You will paddle the rainbow of foam away with your hands
Toward the steps at the entrance.

You will slide like a tile's lustre
In effusive sadness,
And the steam released will dissolve
Over the opened, spotless sea.

XIV

Так заканчивается история дельфинария
И всех его братьев в наушниках,
Которые отстрелялись и сняли пробки с ушей.

Лишь мальки мелькают у арок —
У входа крови нашей, освеженной и вечной.

1982–1985

XIV

Thus ends the history of the dolphinarium
And of all its brothers in earphones,
Who are done and have taken the plugs from their ears.

Only the minnows are left to flit around the archways—
At the entrance to our blood, refreshed and everlasting.

GJ / JT / RS / MY

Балтийские отражения

Е.Т.

Как дневные прогулки,
Далеки острова.
И шаги твои осторожны,
Чтобы след не оставить в мире.

Там морская даль над домами,
Чаек гулкие поплавки,
И вечерняя не молкнет заря,
Словно Альтдорфера битва,
Стянувшись пучком к горизонту.

Здесь природа света чиста.
Световые координаты
На лице твоем прижились.
Но всегда над молчаньем твоим и моря
Красота твоего лица.
И радуги распущенный хвостик,
Угасший за лесом.

Лишь вода отступает,
Проходя по соленым колосьям,
Рядом с памятниками,
Где дети играют,
Ударяя мячом в свое отражение в постаменте.

Мелют все так же соль муки или денег
Мельницы над простором морским,
И радары, словно мельницы ветряные,
За избой на поляне.

Baltic Reflections

for E.T.

Like walks in daytime
The islands are far away.
And your footsteps are careful
To leave no trace in the world.

There, seascapes spread over houses,
The bobble of resonant seagulls,
And the sunset never goes quiet,
Gathering itself into a funnel
As in Altdorfer's "Battle."

Here, the nature of light is pure.
The coordinates of light
Found a home in your face.
But the beauty of that face
Floats forever over your silence and the silence of the sea.
And the rainbow's loosened braid
Disentangles above the forest.

Only the water recedes
Over the salty blades of grass
Alongside monuments
Where children are playing
Bouncing a ball against their reflections in pedestals.

Just as before, mills above the sea's expanse
Grind the salt of money or flour,
And the radars turn like windmills
In the clearing behind the log cabin.

Только ветер кружит
Сквозь ажурные крылья,
Только дети шлепают мячик
И прячут его в ячейку руки.

1985–1986

Only wind keeps circling
Through the gauzy wings;
Only children keep bouncing the ball
And hiding it in the hollow of a hand.

JT / BH

* * *

Выходящие из этой зимы, люди кажутся тоньше,
Из туманного белого мрака,
Где сколоты, словно колбы, льдины подобием матовым молока...
Вырастают оне на автобусной остановке
        в щетине бензиновой, но не новой,
В синей саже,
В новых тенях полинялых,
В длинных полах пальто серо-финских
И храня поставленный на ручник затаенный
        свой голос,—
Это глас их из сна
И глазница пророка проросшего,
Словно льнувшие к людям лунки семян,
        что проклюнулись вдруг на сером окне.
Из отросшего за зиму меха пальто
Ничего не извлечь нам хорошего
Не излечит ничто нас от пасмурной робкой всегда доброты.

1992

* * *

People seem thinner, from this winter emerging,
From the foggy white gloom,
Where matte milky ice blocks chip and splinter like beakers...
These blocks grow up at the bus stop,
    in stubble, not new, but polluted by petrol,
In blue soot,
In new faded shadows,
In long tails of Finnish-gray coats,
And keeping safe their secreted voice that's placed
    on the hand-brake—
It's their voice from dreams,
And a prophet's eyesocket, springing up,
Like those crescents of seed that cling to people,
    seeds that suddenly sprouted on a gray windowsill.
From a coat's fur grown longer over winter
Nothing good can be gained,
Nothing will cure us of this ever-diffident, overcast kindness.

JT / BH / RS / MY

australis
(смотрящей сквозь море)

Та полотняная вода

(взгляд не отводя от южных всех морей и океанов)

возникла вдруг опять
вспомнила ты как полоскала

там где на воды скатерти не стелили

здешний фестиваль развеян
роздана поверхность празднеств и убранств
и темноту волос убрав с лица
ты словно снова взглянешь
в отраженье священных северных рек
под сумрачным обрывом
где прежде полотно ты полоскала

и нынешние флаги трепетные что тебе теперь видны
с полосками морскими колыханий
в них скрыты рыбы лед на глубине
ракушки, крабы и кораллы

но та полотняная вода
ласкала твои руки
так к ней прикасалась ты
как будто ты ее стирала

светлела давняя вода

морщины исчезали

и видишь что меж пальцев
выступили в воде истинные созвездия иные

australis
    (to her, who looks through the sea)

That linen water

    (without averting eyes from all southern seas and oceans)

  again you suddenly rose up
  remembering how you were washing, rinsing

    there, where no tablecloths were laid out on the waters

      the local festival has been dispersed
        the trappings of celebrations and decorations distributed
          and having from your face brushed dark of hair
      it's like you'll glance again
        at the reflection of sacred northern rivers
          under the somber twilight cliff
        where you once washed your linen sheet

  and today's trembling banners which you now see
      with sea-like quivering stripes
        in these lie hidden fish, ice buried in the deep
          seashells, crabs, and corals

      but that linen water
        caressed your hands
          the way you touched it
            as if it were what you were washing

        that long-ago water was becoming bright

    its wrinkles vanishing

    and then you see between your fingers
    true new constellations rising in the water

Павлин и Феникс и ближний к нам Центавр

вышиты морские знаки

и тебе склоненной
в отраженьи виден Южный Крест

2008

The Peacock, the Phoenix, and—closest to us—the Centaur

embroidered—these signs of the sea

and visible to you, as you lean over,
the Southern Cross in the reflection

JT / BH / MY / RS

Пьеса

Две поэтессы напротив друг друга
На табуретках
Покачиваясь

Изображая июньскую встречу
Ту полутайную
Перед самой войной
При немногих свидетелях
В комнате восьмиметровой
«Был ли паркет, это надо проверить
Или только партер марьино-рощинской пыли»,—
Так говорил режиссер им,
Что рассадил их по двум сторонам
                                  комнаты
«Собственных стихов не читайте,
        но держите их наготове
           рядом с речью...
Перед собою протяните руку
        с большим бумажным листком
        на которых написано их имя...»

Он предложил им одеться
         в старые водолазки
Чтобы осталось, не утонув, в безликом том трикотаже
         только лицо.

«Вы играйте лицами
        белыми, как листки,
       на которых еще
       не написаны глаза и ресницы
    играйте хотя бы с чистого древесного листа липы»

«Лицо поэта,— так он им говорил,—
        в моем представленьи — лишь цветная

A Play

Two poetesses face to face
On stools
Rocking back and forth

Portraying that June meeting
Semi-secret
Just before the war
In presence of scant witness
In a room of eight square meters
"Was it a hardwood floor, this needs to be determined,
Or just the dusty orchestra seats of Maryina Roshcha"
That's what they heard the director say to them,
He who placed them in opposite corners of the
                                room
"Don't read your own poems
        but keep them ready
                beside the scripted speech...
Stretch your hands out ahead holding
                a large sheet of paper
                on which their names are written..."

He suggested as costumes
                old turtleneck sweaters
So that only the face would not be submerged
                in that featureless fabric.

"Act with your faces alone,
        white as blank pages
        on which eyes and lashes
        are not yet painted,
    play from blank sheet of the linden tree's new leaf"

"A poet's face," he told them,
        "in my understanding, is but a colorful

неуловимая ткань, по которой войною
времен проходят лица встреченных им»

«Можно курить?»

«Нет, не нужно. Потерпите.»

«Для кого мы играем? И что значит «играть»?»

«Вы остановочный пункт...что вполне достаточно...
    или безостановочный...   времен
тот пунктир, откуда
    исходят волны ветра
        от ваших волос
    в прошлое, к тому дню...
или в будущее»

«Но продолжим...
Именно он воплощает других
Имя его —
        это мозаика благодарных имен других
Но именно им
Он обязан всем
Потому что они — его воплощенье»

Приблизительно так бормотал он им в уши...
Обдавая свежим дыханьем
Внушая инструкции, отвлеченные,
                как реклама лаванды.

«Изображая другого
        мы имя держим свое
            словно маску перед собой
                но написано на нем имя чужое»
И он выдал им листки,
            прикрепленные на длинных планках

and elusive fabric, over which pass the faces
of those they've encountered, like the battles of times past."

"Can we smoke?"

"No, you shouldn't. Wait a little."

"Who is the audience? And what does 'play' mean?"

"You are the point where the train stops... that's enough to know...
            or does not stop...   that dotted line
        of time from which
            wind gusts
                through your hair
            into the past, back to the day of that meeting...
        or into the future."

"But let's go on...
It is just it that embodies others
Its name—
        A mosaic of the thankful names of others
But it owes precisely everything
To them
Because they are its embodiment."

This is more or less what he murmured in their ears,
Breathing fresh words,
Filling them with instructions as abstract
                        as an ad for lavender.

"Impersonating the other
        you hold up your name
            before you as a mask
                but it is the name of another."
And he gave them sheets of paper
            fastened to long slats

похожий на белый веер
написав слова
на одном «Ахматова», на другом «Цветаева»
«Так вы станете двойным анонимом»,—
он внушал им.

Изображая других
на табуретках пригнувшись
в черном своем трикотаже.

«Ваш диалог отдаленно может напоминать
допрос»

«Кто же кого допрашивал?»

«Никто никого
и при том—обе друг друга
эта встреча, в которой
воплотилась вся жизнь
это пьеса... потому что они играли
встречей своей всю-то жизнь нашу...
все свидания безымянные
при понятых... при свидетелях
чьи лица едва различимы в рембрандтовской темноте

ведь все, кто искал другого...
встретились в этой комнатке
и кто, говорил утвердительно
тот вопрошал
и смотрел на себя
сквозь драгоценные глаза другого»

Вечер... нескончаемый вечер июньский

«Помните... в последний раз
встреча их на этой земле

                    resembling white fans
           on one he had written
"Akhmatova" and on the other, "Tsvetaeva"
"This will make you anonymous doubles,"
                    he impressed upon them.

Impersonating others,
           huddled on your stools
           in your black jerseys.

"Your dialogue might remind us a little of
                    an interrogation."

"Who was interrogating whom?"

"No one interrogated anyone
                    and even so—each interrogated the other
           it's a meeting in which
           a whole lifetime was embodied
                    it's a play... because through this meeting
                    our entire life was played out...
           all those anonymous meetings
           in the presence of appointed witnesses
with barely distinguishable faces in Rembrandt-like darkness

                    because all those who were seeking another...
           met in that little room
           and whoever made statements
                    was actually asking questions
                    and was looking at himself
           through the priceless eyes of another"

Evening... a never-ending evening in June

"Remember... this is the last
                    time they meet on earth

но здесь на дощатом полу нашей комнаты
на подмостках, верней, на
мостках расставанья
вы напомнить должны
что их встреча еще состоится.
Вы не играйте
Ту первую ордынскую безымянную встречу
Вы играйте вторую
где-то в Марьиной роще
а Александровском переулке
Но главное — вы играйте себя
Играйте свидетелей марьиных рощ
облаков волокнистых стад над Москвой
над московским июнем
запечатлевшим как паспорт
всех нас...
но тех неизвестных соседей
кто спал в других коммунальных комнатах
как молодой сосняк
не знает никто»

Две поэтессы в черном
Начинают играть
тихо проявляясь лицом в темном воздухе
они могут изображать все, что хочет любая из рук

«Вы поймите... им не играть предстояло—
рыдать...
трубным голосом звать...
и рубашки шить
из подорожника ниток...
Или играть только небо
за небольшим окном
играть тот июнь
что мгновенно ушел тогда незамеченный

here, on these floorboards of this room,
of this stage, or more precisely,
on the makeshift planks of parting
you must remind the audience
that their meeting is yet to take place.
Don't play
That first anonymous meeting on the Ordynka
Play the second one
somewhere in the district of Maryina Roshcha
in Aleksandrovsky Alley
But most importantly—play yourselves
Play the witnesses to the groves of Maryina Roshcha,
flocks of curly clouds over Moscow
over Moscow's June
which like passport photos recorded
all of us...
but those unknown neighbors
who slept in the other communal apartment rooms
like a stand of young pines
remain anonymous,"

Two poetesses dressed in black
Begin to act
faces quietly emerging from the dark air
they can portray anything, whatever either hand desires

"Understand... they were not destined to act—
but to weep...
to call with a trumpeting voice...
and to weave shirts
from threads of roadside broadleaf...
Or to play just the sky
beyond a small window
to play that June
which came and then went unnoticed in an instant

Поймите,
     вы играете монумент
       той встречи
   но играйте так, будто
       она была репетицией
     встречи вашей здесь и сейчас»

«Дверь откройте,— он сказал
     чтобы воздух
    входил постоянно
чтобы вы ощущали живой сквозняк,
       озноб на известковых своих локтях
Вы воплощение их
     они остановились, проходя, в вашем взгляде
     в этой комнате со свежими окнами...»
Обе синхронно отерли глаза
     при пробужденьи
     от слез или снов

И продолжали молча играть

2002

Understand,
     you are playing a monument
       to that meeting
   but you must act as if
     it were a rehearsal
    of your meeting here and now"

"Open the door," he said,
   "so that the air
  will enter continuously
so that you feel the fresh draft
    a chill on your chalky elbows
You embody these two
    walking past, they paused in your gaze
     in this room with its windows opening to green..."
They both wiped their eyes
   upon awakening
    from tears or dreams

And silently went on with the play

JT / BH

71

К появлению собрания стихов Геннадия Айги

Семитомник твой —
Ствол застенчиво выступает из тьмы
              вослед за другим стволом

Лес становится деревом снова
Поле горизонтом безграничную обозначает страницу

С чистой страницы
Мы читаем твой снег

Словно одну снежинку...

Тает — не тает
Но именно та
остается как слово
              Твое

2009

On the Release of a Collection of Poems by Gennady Aygi

Your collected poems in seven books:
One tree trunk after another shyly emerges
                                        from the dark

The forest becomes a tree again
A field's horizon defines a borderless page

On a blank page
We read your snow

Like a single snowflake...

It melts—or—it doesn't
But just that one
Remains as a word
        Yours

JT / BH

30 апреля

Вызвать меж забвенья вещей образ
Алена твой
Здесь в средостеньи берез
Аляповатых губ примкнувшего
трутовика
Шумом шоссе неясным оплакана
Высота сосны горечь-даль
сталь давняя неба —
Обещание верное

Бутоны черных копий
на углах железных оград
И несмела несметная
Зелень
пробирается первый раз
на парад земли
и в повторе как песня
вытянет, вызволит во всю длину   жизнь
жизнь твою вечную

2010

April 30th

To evoke, amid the oblivion of things, your image
Alyona
Here in the colonnade of birches
The clumsy lips of the attached
        shelf mushroom
The highway's indistinct murmur
Mourns the height of the pine, the bitter distance,
        The ancient steel of the sky—
A faithful promise

Black spears on the corners
    of cast iron fences bear buds
    And timidly, the myriad host of
    Greenery
    creeps through for the first time
to join the earth's parade
        and as in a song repeating the refrain
        it will stretch to full span and set free   a life
    your life—eternal

JT / BH / MY

75

Лица в метро

Плавающие   слева иль справа
   сплавы   их листьев
        на лацканах
  металлических

             Объемы их   объемна их
     славы их глаз
            листва живая

       не говорили   их глаза
      но порознь   каждый
      жили   глядел и уходил
             не уходил
         в свою сторону света
   света   пролетающего за черным окном

2010

Faces in the Metro

Floating   on the left or the right
  the alloy   of their leaves
    on metallic
   lapels

       Their volumes voluminous
  the living leaves
      of their eyes' splendor

    their eyes   unspeaking
   but separately   each one
   lived   gazed and left
        never leaving
      for its own side of the world's
  light   flying past a black window

JT / BH

Переулок

На перекрестке ночном
                    Трехпрудного   где разделяется   он
На Ермолаевский и Благовещенский

            ты стоял тогда и сейчас

Направо   налево   ль пойдешь —
        словно два свежих отворота —
        воротника у форменки
        отклонены во тьму

направо ли — в Благовещенский
        где закрыв глаза   снится все тихий утренний
                            шелест сумки холщовой
            направо ли   там где   казармы и за
                            стеклами лица безмолвны

        налево ли   где каштаны светятся над посольством со
                                    странным страны
окончанием
                    на   «агвай» или «угвай»

        Но не слишком ли обнажена   там
            улицы   Жолтовского   улицы
                        будущей
            в повороте ночном книжная эта желчная
                        желтизна

Кто передоверил   перепроверил   кто   не   переуступил

                на пороге осеннем

The Alley

At night on the crossroads
                where   Trekhprudny   divides
into Yermolaevsky and Blagoveshchensky

        You stood then and are standing now

Whether you go   right   or left
        like the two ends of a collar
            on a school uniform
                inclined toward the dark

if to the right—into Blagoveshchensky alley
        where with eyes closed   one dreams of the quiet rustling
                                    of a canvas-clad bag in the morning
            if to the right   where   the barracks line up
                                    and faces in the windows go silent

        if to the left   where the chestnut trees shine over an embassy
                                    with the strange ending
of a country
                            in   "aguay" or "uguay"

        But is not this bookish jaundiced yellow of
            Zholtovsky   street   the street
                        yet to come
            a bit overexposed   over there
                        in the nighttime turn

Who re-entrusted   re-calibrated   who   did not   re-cede

                    on autumn's threshold

79

свои права
чтобы за всех видеть
и тихо за вас всех сказать

2010

                              his rights
          to see for everyone
          and quietly speak for you all

JT / BH / MY

Памяти Алеши

Где-то под аркой тогда —
    открытой из поля в поле —
    названных Соловьиным проездом
рядом
    белая голубая ячейка-плитка на стене
                дома

            и неправдоподобное чудо
        автомат-телефон   кажется он так назывался?
от той отлетевшей плитки
    я говорил с тобою тогда
    из голоса в голос
        в комнату твою на высоте

    где-то в середине 80-х...
в мае в один из дней твоего рожденья

        вспомнил сейчас...   потому что   прочел у Кавафиса
            упоминание об Аполлонии Таианском

верно...
        я тебе подарил «Жизнеописание Аполлония»

        был я единственный, кто пришел тогда к тебе

    ты отвечал вкрадчиво
    что день рожденья не празднуешь
    но если зайдешь буду рад

            начал читать ты с тех пор
                жизнь Аполлония
        в которую я перестал заглядывать уже в лифте

In Memory of Alyosha [to Alexei Parshchikov]

Somewhere under an arch then—
    opening from one field onto another
called Nightingale Drive
alongside
    the wall of a building with white and blue
                                        tiles

        and an unlikely miracle
        a payphone   that's what it was called?
near those chipped tiles
    I spoke with you that night
        my voice merging with yours
        in your room high overhead

    sometime in the mid-eighties...
in May on one of your birthdays

        I think of it now   having just   read Cavafy
            alluding to Apollonius of Tyana

it's true...
        I gave you "The Life of Apollonius"

    I was the only one who came to you then

    you answered evasively
    that you never celebrated birthdays
    but you'd be happy for me to come by

            since then, you've been reading
                "The Life of Apollonius,"
        which I had already stopped skimming in the elevator

и затем не смотрел

потому что она в надежном взоре
и читаешь ее только ты

теперь ты ушел — и я знаю
что книга открыта и мне
просто теперь я могу приподнять эти строки
полные тайн и чудес
Но что есть   не стоящие одного слова
истинного   другого
чудеса и тайны?

и все же все то, что хранили глаза твои
на оборотной стороне
взгляда —
попробуем собирать   — твое зрение
рассеянное для нас
(пусть на странице описания жизни)
затерянное среди ясеневской листвы

Прикрывая глаза, я отчетливо вижу твой свет.

2009

and didn't look into again

because it was now for your trusted eye
and yours alone to read

now you have left for good—and I know
the book is open for me as well
so now I can lift up those verses
full of secrets and wonders
But what are   wonders and secrets
that aren't worth   a true   other's
single word?

and still, all that your eyes preserved,
on the far side of your
gaze—
let us try to gather it   —your vision
is for us dispersed
(even if only on a page from a life)
lost among the leaves in Yasenevo

Closing my eyes, I clearly see your light.

JT / BH

85

* * *

Убаюкает нас дорога
В люльке с девятнадцатого века.
Он хотел бы пожрать пространство
Да видно не в железного коня корм.
Мы хранимся в поездной колыбели
Словно красавица в начале бесконечного сна.

2014

* * *

The road will rock us to sleep
In a bassinet from the nineteenth century.
It would devour the expanse
But in vain the fodder for the iron horse.
We're kept safe in the cradle of the train—
A fair maiden at the start of an endless dream.

RS / MY

* * *

Все под голубыми одеялами вагонными
С улыбками разной стойкости
Витают в своих небесах.

Сон повальный нас всех поразил
Кажется, не может быть направленья во сне
И все же
Ледяная всем предстоит стрела.

Однорукая жизнь маячит
Милосердия просит, и мы
Отдаем ей то немногое, что у нас есть во сне.

2014

* * *

All of them under blue wagon blankets
With smiles of varied stability
Soaring in their personal skies.

An epidemic of dream laid us flat
It seems dreams can't have a course
And even so
A bolt of ice awaits us all.

A one-armed life looms indistinctly,
Asks for mercy, and we
Return it what little we have in our dreams.

RS / MY

Памяти Аркадия Драгомощенко

Аркадий, можно ль найти ненужный
   какой-нибудь в мире предмет

      но не дается
   все у нас приспособлено
      все вокруг сподручно, все под рукой
      все говорит и о том, и о сем
      все задает не вопрос, а ответ
   не обнаружить   совсем постороннюю лишнюю
вещь — это был бы ковчег для тебя

         но все они сочтены
         все подшиты для дела
         все пущены в ход или в рост

      нет ни щепочки, что была бы ненужной
                        кому-нибудь
   но где — для тебя?
ты бы создал ее сам в своесильном
зрении, ты бы ей удивился
   но для удивленья теперь —
            нет-мир без тебя

   тише и тоньше сейчас
         словно бы все
   лезвия слез своих обнажили
   но все же оставили мир без надреза
и некуда закатиться, исчезнуть невинной вещи
         все они, все они здесь,
                  сочтены

In Memory of Arkadii Dragomoshchenko

Arkadii, where in the world
   is there an object without use?

      but it's elusive
    everything here is put to use
      everything around is handy, all of it at hand
    everything refers to something else
    everything gives answers without questions
    one can discover no   completely superfluous extraneous
thing—though that would've been an ark for you

     but all these things are counted
     all of them filed for the brief
     all of them put into action or gaining interest

    not a scrap that someone wouldn't need
                for something
  but what's left for you?
you would have created it yourself from your own
self-powered vision, you would have marveled at it
  but the only marvel now
         is a no-world without you

   it's thinner and quieter now
      as if everyone
  bared the blades of their tears
  yet left the world without an incision
there's nowhere for an innocent thing to disappear
      to roll under something, here all of them
     every single one is counted

вижу, лишь легкая краснота
           на месте том, где стоял ты
   но через такой порез
       не произойдет ничего

мы соберем, собираем к себе
       всех, кто летел над настурцией
   всех   кто
       по ту сторону ранки

2012

I see only a lightly blushing abrasion
           in the place where you stood
      but through such a fissure
         nothing can come to pass

   we will gather, we gather to us
         all those who flew over the nasturtiums
      all those   who exist
            on the other side of the cut

JT / BH / MY

JULIA TRUBIKHINA-KUNINA: How did it happen that you, a physicist who had graduated from the Moscow Institute of Physics and Technology, a PhD in physics and author of more than 150 scientific publications, live a parallel life as "Poet Vladimir Aristov"? Or, perhaps, these are simply two independent, separate lives—"physics" and "lyrics," to use the well-known Soviet juxtaposition of the 1960s?

VLADIMIR ARISTOV: For a poet to do something else, other than poetry, is normal and examples abound. At a certain "sublime" level, in the case of physics and mathematics (and I don't mean this just as a profession), there was, of course, something more important. It seems to me that the most well-known cultural juxtaposition of the Soviet 1960s ("physics" versus "lyrics") in reality is not a juxtaposition but a relationship at some very deep level. Actually, one need not come up with a new philosophy here: a holistic *weltanschauung* since antiquity never juxtaposed these different ways of cognition. For example, music and mathematics were not separated in medieval education and both were considered integral parts of a single process of acquiring knowledge. And even in high school, literature lessons and math or physics lessons alternated and coexisted peacefully. So if we think of this process of acquiring knowledge as continuing beyond high school, we see nothing strange in one's desire to entertain such different subjects as poetry and physics. One just needs to feel oneself immersed in the process of cognition, in which various ways of vision and expression exist. As a high school student, I was enchanted with the beauty of math—with the problems going beyond the boring school curriculum where everything is known in advance and everything has an answer. I was enchanted with the new, unsolved problems, which suddenly opened up the world as if it were completely new, and here undoubtedly lies a kinship with poetry. The "insurmountable" beauty of a complex math problem helped me discover—in the tension of finding the answer—some distant links to the entire enormous world. To a large extent, this interest was of an aesthetic nature. The beauty of science, first and foremost of its methods rooted in mathematics and theoretical physics, is a little-studied area that shares certain aspects with the much more developed area of aesthetics of poetry.

As far as difference in ways of expression is concerned, then yes, this requires a certain artistic flexibility. I cannot judge how successful I am at playing several different roles (I would assume there exist some more successful "performers"). However, I would have achieved nothing at all without interest in both subjects. I have realized perhaps only 25 percent of all I conceived of. Such ineffectual output is the price paid for the attempt to exist in several spaces at once. On the other hand, I get bored with existing in one space only: I get bored quickly and this leads to zero output. To illustrate such abstract musings, I'd like to share a recent poem. Sure, it is ironic to some extent, but it does provide an echo of, if not an answer to, the question:

Manysided Life

> *But unfortunately, you are a busboy at the*
> *buffet on board of the peaceful ship called*
> *"Guatemala."*
> —Alexander Vertinsky

I might easily be a scholar,
except I would have to study too hard.
I might easily be a poet,
but I would have to be too idle.
I can be neither one nor the other.
On vacation too
all I can do is teach and work
(which rules out being a pirate
even in imagination)
and like snow, soft snow, teach everyone,
myself first of all,
moving from image to image
and at it full-time.

[BH]

Existing in two mutually independent courses of life allows for feeling oneself not divided, but sort of multiplied. This "shining through" of different images is, for me, an example of *idem-forma*.

JTK: Tell me about your early years. What was your family like? Who got you into poetry? Do you hear poetry in anybody's voice?

VA: My parents were geologists—my father was a full professor at the Moscow Geological Prospecting Institute. From them perhaps comes my wanderlust, and not only in its purely geographical sense. At the same time, from them comes also love for books and reading. Our home (to be precise, a rather large room in a communal apartment) was overflowing with various books. Even though poetry was just a fraction of those thousands of books, it was meaningful for me from early on. I clearly hear the voice of my grandmother on my father's side, who lived with us: she sang lullabies to me and my brother, usually in the afternoon, before an after-lunch nap. Among others, she sang us songs written to the poems of Ivan Nikitin and Nikolai Nekrasov. My mother definitely had a knack for literature and she herself was very good at writing. I hear her favorite lines of poetry in her voice, for example, Alexander Blok's "Oh Spring, infinite, boundless..." or Valery Bryusov's "I am the head of kings and king Esarhaddon..." My father was stricter on the outside, less lyrical, but sometimes he recited what had struck him most in his youth—Mayakovsky or perhaps Eduard Bagritsky's "The Lay of Opanas"... So I absorbed something from them as a child, and now these voices are alive in me.

Once, as a young man, I discovered my mother's notebook, in which she and her friends wrote down poetry from memory. This was when she worked in Norilsk. (During World War II she worked as a free hire in a geological expedition affiliated with the Norilsk nickel plant, which was actually under the auspices of NKVD, the Soviet secret police. They saw gulag prisoners, including Lev Gumilev.) In that notebook, I read poetry by authors I knew and some I had never heard of. Among them, I read for the first time two poems by Pasternak—one early poem, still clearly influenced by Symbolism but at the same time marked by Pasternak's original style of much more specific and tangible details ("I dreamt of autumn in the window's twilight..."). The second poem completely entranced me, especially as my reading of it coincides for me with twilight in our dark corner window and snow outside. It had a mistake—"There will be no one at home" instead of "in the house"—and this is how I remember it. There were also some other mistakes, understandable because all the poems were written down from memory, and perhaps by more than one person. But back then I perceived that first mistake as daring poetic license and a great innovation: because of that replacement, written in my mother's hand, the lack of a full rhyme was compensated for by the assonances in the middle of the next stanza, contrary to the strict rules of syllabo-tonic versification. (Pasternak would not have accepted that).[1] Only much later did I learn of the correct version, and at first I even refused to accept it. With these examples, I am trying to illustrate how complicated my "coming to poetry" was: it was difficult to find real poetry but, on the other hand, such oblique paths have preserved a link for me to unique images and voices.

JTK: There are twenty years between the time you started writing poetry in the end of the 1960s and you first publications in the second half of the 1980s. Who was and is in your literary circle? What is your connection to the poet Alexei Parshchikov? What did the members of your circle have in common? Were there some common poetics and aesthetic principles?

VA: My high school classmates were my first proper "literary circle." I am still friends with some of them. A few of them wrote poetry but never sought a literary career, though there were some real connoisseurs of poetry among them.

---

1 The Pasternak poem Aristov refers to begins, "There will be no one in the house..." ("Nikogo ne budet v dome..."). His mother recorded the last word of the line as "doma," creating the slant rhyme which Pasternak would not have allowed.

The first eight years after graduating from high school, when I realized that poetry was something extremely important to me, I wrote in almost complete isolation. Of course there were a few select friends: I dared to show them my first experiments. But I did not make any attempts to penetrate "official literature." In part, that was due to shyness and because I saw that I still needed to perfect my style; but it was also due to my understanding that my literary interests and preferences diverged sharply from Soviet poetic practice. (I was right about that.) If Jack London's neurotic protagonist, Martin Eden, could even have imagined the time that lay ahead of us—my fellow poets and I—with no hope of official self-realization! Yet, twenty years is not such a long time... Poets of the previous Soviet generations must have had a sober understanding of what it was like to have no hope at all.

My fellow poets and I started publishing when we were around 37—an age when some poets, Pushkin for example, had finished their literary careers. In the middle of the 1970s, in college at MGU, I attended a literary club and met some interesting authors; still, that literary club (known as Igor Volgin's literary seminar) seemed to a large extent "retrospective" for me: the new forms and poetic ideas that I was interested in were not well-accepted in that noble "nature preserve" of literary tradition. In this sense, Kirill Kovaldzhi's literary studio in the early 1980s was just the opposite: there, explicitly and implicitly, most unusual and innovative experiments were welcome. However, all these things are, so to say, "extraliterary"; most important was the internal work, which I discussed with the like-minded people I discovered in the late 1970s and early 1980s: Ivan Zhdanov and Alexei Parshchikov. Later, other poets also became important to me: Yuriy Arabov and Arkadii Dragomoshchenko. I met Nikolai Kononov in Leningrad in the late 1980s, and this was very important to me too. It is hard to tell the whole story in a few words. There is an opinion that nothing united those very different writers except the time and place they shared, but it is still no accident that they had chosen each other: that "selection" of like-minded people had been going on for many years. In my article, "Notes on 'Meta'," I tried to outline the new poetic idea (its outlines had to be not only seen, but created), which spread out over a rather narrow but growing circle of poets.

JTK: You've won many literary prizes, including the Alexei Kruchenykh prize (1993) and the Andrei Bely prize (2008). In addition to poetry, you also write prose and dramatic works (such as "Theater of One Philosopher" about the Russian philosopher Gustav Shpet, who died in the Stalinist purges of 1937). Your novel, Predictions of an Eyewitness, *reminded me of Nabokov by the loving attention you pay to seemingly minute but, in actuality, uniquely important details of life. How do poetry and prose co-exist (or perhaps bounce off each other) for you? Are you drawing closer to the idea of writing a "big Russian novel"? If so, what would it be like? What can prose give you that poetry cannot?*

VA: My interests develop along different paths; I am drawn in different directions. It is interesting to experience both the gravitational pull between prose and poetry, as well as their bouncing off each other. I have long been trying to determine for myself the differences between "lyrical poetry," "prose," and "drama" and to understand why each attracts me in its own way. I wrote about it in an essay which was published recently in *NLO* (*New Literary Observer*). In a few words: the affirmation of "I" is central to poetry, of "you"—to prose, and of "us"—to drama. I am interested in various sides of my relationship to the Other; the Other for me is not only an object of communication or reflection, but a new, unknown, future world that is waiting to be experienced by each person. I'm drawn to exploring this world in various ways. Obviously, poetry, prose, and drama are all separate realms, and each demands huge efforts to be penetrated.

JTK: Your theoretical ideas, which you have described with a Latin term idem-forma, are not entirely clear to me. As far as I can see, this is an umbrella term to describe a certain unity of a variety of different texts, not necessarily literary texts, in their formal manifestations—where disparate works, at the first glance not connected in any way, can meet.

What do you mean by this unity of references? Some sort of aerial scaf-
foldings, a web of associations—like in Mandelstam's poetics, when one
distant reference can draw to life a whole cluster of images, including
those created by completely different poets? Or is it some sort of epistemo-
logical unity in nature—that of humanities, science, theology? The poet
Andrei Tavrov has described your idem-forma *as "homonyms of being";*
he points out your adherence to the Nietzschean idea of eternal recur-
rence, that is, essentially, repetition. Can you give an example?

VA: The foundation of the notion of *idem-forma* is in simple, tra-
ditional Christian (or generally, religious) ideas of love for the
Other. But to transfer from the metaphysical to the philosophical
level, the form of such a relationship to the Other needs to be
developed. From the vantage point of literature, of poetry, this
means an attempt to find new ways and modes of expression,
not so much by kinship but rather by "identification." From the
vantage point of rhetoric this implies developing such notions as
metabola.

"To be different" without expunging the difference—this might be
a motto of this new and therefore unfathomable quest. Discussing
Nietzschean "eternal return" would require too much time; it is
too complicated to explain in a few words. It would be better to
use examples from literature proper. Discovering obscured rela-
tionships between pairs of literary works (poems, novels, etc.),
which are not related on the surface level, allows us to develop and
at the same time illustrate the method of *idem-forma.* In many of
my essays, I have tried to clarify the similarities and differences of
this method from the classical comparativist one and from more
recent intertextualist approaches. For example, in the dissimilar
worlds created by William Faulkner and Andrei Platonov, one
finds elements of amazing structural similarity, matching struc-
tural patterns, in which the unique is capable of influencing the
universal and "structuring" it, as it were. These matching patterns
can be manifested in literal coincidences on the very surface of
things. To give you just one example of what I am talking about
here: for Faulkner, the name "John Sartoris" has many meanings,

including an autobiographical one. Amazingly, in the distant artistic world of Platonov a similar name belongs to one of the main characters of the novel *Happy Moscow*, the inventor and engineer Semen Sartorius.

However the structural similarities are much more intricate and complex than simple coincidences. Take, for example, the two fundamental works by Faulkner and Platonov—their novels *The Sound and the Fury* and *The Foundation Pit*, respectively. They exhibit a very curious relationship. In them, certain superficial coincidences correlate with parallel internal artistic meanings. Faulkner's *The Sound and the Fury* came out on October 7, 1929, just prior to the collapse of the New York stock market and the beginning of the Great Depression. Platonov started writing *The Foundation Pit* at the end of 1929, the year of the so called "Great Break"—the end of the New Economic Policy and Stalin's ascent to power. The novel was completed in April 1930 and not published in the USSR until nearly 60 years later. Even though both works are filled with almost abstract symbolism, the connections to their time and external circumstances are obvious. The connection is not so much factual as structural, as the texts convey a torturous state of being. Thus in Faulkner, the sophisticated Quentin Compson seeks death; he is a "lover of death," as Faulkner puts it. The idea of death and suicide also haunts the engineer Prushevsky, the most self-reflective character in Platonov's novel. When Prushevsky thinks of dying, he plans to write his sister a letter the next morning and buy a stamp. A stamp and a letter are also images from the last hours of Quentin's life. Accidental details that the two novels have in common form a scintillating, pulsing surface of consistency and pattern. Faulkner spoke of his novel as a tragedy of two fallen women, Caddy and her daughter. *The Foundation Pit* is also a tragedy of two women—Nastya and her mother. In Platonov, this tragedy is real, literal death, not metaphorical as in Faulkner, but the paired image of women, mother and daughter, is used in both novels to convey the meaning of rupture in the world.

The motif of fury and prophetic insanity correlates in Faulkner with a wider tradition in world literature—with Dostoyevsky, with Shakespeare's tragedies... The title, of course, refers to "Macbeth." When Macbeth is at the edge of death and learns about the death of Lady Macbeth, he goes into his famous soliloquy about the essence of human life: "...it is a tale told by an idiot, full of sound and fury, signifying nothing." The meaning of "fury" in the worlds of Faulkner and Platonov ranges from rage and the insanity of the world and the characters to the elevating breakthrough that carries one beyond the routine of the everyday. For both Faulkner and Platonov, "fury" is also the white-hot hyper-intensity of burning, the insane but blissful passion in which a gleam of eternity manifests itself in an instantaneous flash of life. (In Russian, *yaryi* [furious] and *yarkii* [bright] derive from the same stem.) There are multiple examples of the use of the word "fury" in both novels. Fury or rage at finding oneself in the grip of being is the key philosophical category in both authors' oeuvres, hence the passionate intensity of the worlds of their characters.

JTK: Can you describe your poetics? Is metaphor for you, as it was for Parshchikov, the central and defining element of your poetics? What is your place in the Metarealist/Meta-metaphorist movement?

VA: To be fair, Parshchikov's metaphor might not be the most important thing in his poetics. His metaphors are what jump out at you and what a trained ear is accustomed to hearing. In actuality, his poetics is comprised of a multiplicity of sophisticated devices, not so easy to notice and difficult to define. I say this because it is easier to get away with an expected self-definition, which might not actually reflect anything. (I could define my poetics as the "poetics of *idem-forma*," but this might be too general.) Also, perhaps you know yourself less than someone else. A mirror shows a distorted image—not because you see yourself in reverse, but because it is the way others see you. You see yourself this way only partly; you can also see yourself from within. And this makes all the difference. So a self-definition of one's poetics would be either a simplistic declaration or a very imprecise subjective testimony, which might have little to do with what others see and hear. Subjectively, continuous chains of sound seem to play an important role in "my poetics"; they seem to wind around one another and create a somewhat monotonous rhythm. The meter in my poems is even more monotonous than in traditional syllabotonic verse, but there are also constant breaking points, a constant invasion of images that negate the "high tide" of this superficially monotonous rhythm.

Perhaps there is an "intimate metaphysics," expressed only in the language of poetry, which gets vulgarized when talked about abstractly. Therefore one can say only a few general words about "Meta"—its participants did not seek to articulate manifestos, even though there are plenty of disparate statements. Most important, perhaps, is to see through their poetry a gleam of the world of the future, in which there is no destruction or disappearance, and to overcome fear before that world in order to understand the problems one will face over there, which we cannot even imagine now. "The fear of immortality"—this is what defines the state of our suicidal age from the vantage point of Meta poetry. There is a truism that art is necessary while there is death. Metarealism attempted to debunk such claim, even though that might have been a utopian attempt. It attempted to feel Blake's "eternity in an hour" as reality.

All these musings might seem abstract but, it seems to me, they defined, if not always articulated, the situation of Russian poetry in the 1970s, or at least of some poetry—a situation of joy and despair. The literary scene of the Soviet '60s, which often took the shape of poetry read from stage, was replaced in the '70s with poetry from the underground, with all the sickliness this entails but also with all the insights of "undeground people." In the '80s these poets emerged from the underground not quite able to believe their own eyes. For me, the main characteristic of that time is the impossibility of utterance—an accumulation of the energy of inner expression—along with seeking to obtain inner poetic freedom and to open up into the world. Almost a decade of "poetic silence," of going deep into self—these were the Soviet '70s.

To be more specific about myself: until the mid-1970s, with almost a decade of writing poetry under my belt, I had never seen a live poet. It might have been partly due to circumstances, but I also wanted to reach a level that would really open up some new horizons. Every time I thought I had achieved something, it would turn out to be not quite right... The appearance of certain translations of the world's poetry around that time, which one could, at least in part, see as models, contributed to such understanding. I still felt isolated until almost the late '70s, when I had already started hanging out with some poets. It seemed to me that there were no poets who were kindred spirits, or else they were "deeply undercover." This was natural for the late Soviet period: by then people already felt that private life was "allowed," but social connections were ruptured and many existed in their own isolated spaces, as it were. Therefore the appearance of a whole group of such authors at the end of the 1970s struck me as unexpected. I remember their first reading at TsDRI (The Central House of Art Workers) in 1979: Zhdanov, Parshchikov, Eremenko, with Kedrov introducing them. I remember standing in the March sleet on Gorky Street before the reading (I knew before I heard them that they would be those I had been looking for and I was right!) and trembling—not from cold but from anticipation and a sense of kinship for that poetry.

I perceived Zhdanov as my elder brother in poetry. Back in 1977, I had once heard him read his poem "Pain, Stay in the Needle..." and thought that it was the most complex thing I had ever heard; and afterwards I thought that it was also the closest to me. Then, in the sudden silence that followed the reading, the poet Sergei Gandlevsky said: "So... It's good poetry!" You can talk specifically and at length about the various styles of the authors of that group— of Ilya Kutik's epic or of the virtiginous metamorphoses of Andrei Tavrov's images—or you can just pinpoint some first impressions...

Dragomoshchenko is a poet very different from me but there is something in his method and poetic expression in which we truly overlap; Mikhail Epstein called it "continualism," or a depiction of the world without gaps. The most important thing is to find expression for gaps between things, to make connections between real things, to bring forth something that is usually deemed unimportant or peripheral.

Parshchikov, in this sense, is different: for him, all things are lit by some "metaphysical" light; the boundaries between things are palpable but precisely for this reason, all things paradoxically can form "alliances" or be concatenated into "garlands," mutually integrated without fear of losing self. In his poetry, the vivid characteristics of things—and for him, vividness, the visually compelling nature of an image is central—provide a means for formulating a new understanding of Leibniz's monad.

Of the entire Meta circle, Zhdanov is perhaps closest to me because of his metaphysical underpinnings. However, while our metaphysical outlook (which is not and perhaps cannot be explicitly formulated) might be close, our poetry differs a great deal. Zhdanov almost always makes an *eidos* of a thing or notion as his point of departure. The "inviolability" of the essence of a thing or feeling in his poetry strongly affects his readers or audience. I, on the other hand, almost always depart from an empirically palpable object, tangible in its unique specificity. But in the end, I think, there is a connection through *idem-forma*...

JTK: What are you working on now? What would you like to write?

VA: My new book of poetry has recently been published by the publisher Russian Gulliver. It is entitled *Around Our World With a Notebook (Innocent Poems)*. There is a certain democratic simplicity to its form... Little by little, I am writing some new things. Some are the continuation and development of what I did before, but also, it seems to me, there is something completely new in them now: the multiplicity of voices and situations are now condensing in new forms. It is as if it were a trip around our world not just with a notebook, but with some yet unknown tools for recognizing the Other, for getting to know strangers. I have finished (or so it seems) a long poem, "Night Expanses in July." I have been writing it for six years and almost lost hope of finishing it, but it all fell together when I realized that I could place texts on transparent sheets: then the parts started showing through like palimpsests and the meanings of the poem became clear or, literally, transparent... I am trying to put together a book of essays on *idem-forma*, but because I always come up with more and more articles, the process of writing never comes to an end... I also keep trying to put together yet another book of essays that I have written over many years and, perhaps, a small book on Pasternak. Over twenty-five years, I have written a number of essays on his poetry that cumulatively convey the idea of his poetics; I have also spoken a few times about his poetry at the Pasternak museum at his *dacha* in Peredelkino. Generally, what I write and what I would like to write curiously overlap because I have been working on some things for many years, if not decades. As I keep working, the date for finishing all these things seems to become ever more distant rather than closer. For instance, this is the case with my novel, which for the time being has the title *Along the Shining of Rivers*, and whose idea came to me in the early 1970s. I am trying to complete yet another novel, *Mater Studiorum*, and a theatrical piece, for now called "A Memoir." As always, what is needed is more time. Or, perhaps, more focus.

Vladimir Aristov is a poet and physicist. Since his first publications in the late 1980s, Aristov has authored seven books of poetry, a novel, numerous articles and essays, and a play about the Russian philosopher Gustav Shpet, killed by Stalin in the 1930s. Associated with the Metarealist movement, Aristov's poetry and essays have been published in *Nezavisimaia gazeta*, *Arion*, *Vozdukh*, *New Literary Observer (NLO)*, and other Russian literary magazines. He is a recipient of the Alexei Kruchenykh Prize (1993), the Andrei Bely Independent Literary Prize (2008), and the Razlichie (Distinction) Prize in poetry (2016). His work has been included in two U.S. anthologies of postmodern Russian poetry, *The Third Wave* and *Crossing Centuries: The New Generation in Russian Poetry*. He has translated George Seferis and Michael Palmer into Russian and is currently working on a collection of essays entitled *Idem-Forma*.

Julia Trubikhina-Kunina received her Ph.D. in Comparative Literature from New York University and teaches at Hunter College, CUNY. She has translated Susan Howe, Anthony Hecht, and Nathaniel Tarn into Russian, and her own poetry has appeared in several anthologies, including *An Anthology of Contemporary Russian Women Poets* and *Crossing Centuries: The New Generation in Russian Poetry*, and in literary journals such as *Novyi mir*, *Arion*, and *Boundary 2*. She is the author of three books of poetry, as well as many scholarly articles and a book of literary theory and criticism, *The Translator's Doubts: Vladimir Nabokov and the Ambiguity of Translation*.

The Eastern European Poets Series from Ugly Duckling Presse